Vanessa

SAMUEL BARBER

SCHIRMER

W YORK

VANESSA

Opera in Three Acts

MUSIC BY

Samuel Barber

Text By

GIAN CARLO MENOTTI

GERMAN TRANSLATION BY

Otto Maag

Vocal Score

Piano Reduction by the Composer

$10.00

Ed. 2301

(Revised Edition)

G. SCHIRMER, INC.

NEW YORK

Note

G. SCHIRMER, INC.

609 Fifth Avenue

New York 17, N. Y.

VANESSA had its first performance on January 15, 1958, at the Metropolitan Opera House in New York.

VANESSA	ELEANOR STEBER
ERIKA	ROSALIND ELIAS
THE OLD BARONESS	REGINA RESNIK
ANATOL	NICOLAI GEDDA
THE OLD DOCTOR	GIORGIO TOZZI
THE MAJOR-DOMO	GEORGE CEHANOVSKY
A FOOTMAN	ROBERT NAGY

The production was staged by Gian Carlo Menotti and conducted by Dimitri Mitropoulos. Cecil Beaton designed the sets and costumes.

CHARACTERS

VANESSA, a lady of great beauty, in her late thirties . . . . Soprano

ERIKA, her niece, a young girl of twenty . . . . Mezzo-Soprano

THE OLD BARONESS, Vanessa's mother
and Erika's grandmother . . . . Contralto

ANATOL, a handsome young man in his early twenties . . . . Tenor

THE OLD DOCTOR . . . . Baritone

NICHOLAS, the Major-Domo . . . . Bass

FOOTMAN . . . . Bass

The Young Pastor, Servants, Guests, Peasants, their Children, Musicians.

––––––

The action takes place at Vanessa's country house in a northern country about 1905.

Act I.   Scene 1. The drawing room. A night in early winter.
          Scene 2. The same. Sunday morning, a month later.

Act II.   The entrance hall with the ballroom beyond. New Year's Eve.

Act III. Scene 1. Erika's bedroom. A few hours later.
          Scene 2. The drawing room. A late afternoon, a month later.

This is the story of two women, Vanessa and Erika, caught in the central dilemma which faces every human being: whether to fight for one's ideals to the point of shutting oneself off from reality, or compromise with what life has to offer, even lying to oneself for the mere sake of living. Like a sullen Greek chorus, a third woman (the old Grandmother) condemns by her very silence the refusal first of Vanessa, then of Erika, to accept the bitter truth that life offers no solution except its own inherent struggle. When Vanessa, in her final eagerness to embrace life, realizes this truth, it is perhaps too late.

G.C.M.

Vanessa

Text by
Gian Carlo Menotti

Music by
Samuel Barber
(Revised, 1964)

Act I
Scene 1

(A night in early winter in Vanessa's luxurious drawing room. A small table is laid for supper, stage right. All the mirrors in the room and one large painting over the mantelpiece are covered over with cloth. There is a large French window at the back which leads into a darkened jardin d'hiver. Vanessa is sitting by the fire, stage left, her face shadowed by a veil. The Baroness is sitting in front of her and remains immobile throughout the scene until her exit. In the middle of the room a group of servants, headed by Nicholas, the Major-domo, is standing in front of Erika; she is giving them orders, a notebook in her hand. There is a snowstorm outside.)

* A glossary of tempo indications in English, German, and Italian appears at the end of this score.

44349C

A somewhat sustained

again ♩ = 120

Dark and unquiet ♩ = 72

(*Curtain*)

Erika

Er. Po-ta-ge crè-me auxper-les.

Major-domo (*repeats order to servants, speaking*)

M.-D. Po-ta-ge crè-me aux per-les.

*Throughout this score a ⌐——⌐ in the vocal part (although without a *3*) signifies a triplet.

(A butler enters with a lighted candelabra, places it on the dinner-table and leaves.)

2 **Erika**

Er. É-cre-vis-ses à la bor-de-lai-se.

Major-domo

M.-D. É-cre-vis-ses à la bor-de-lai-se.

Vanessa *(without moving)*

Va. Find some-thing bet-ter than that!
Schla-ge was bes-se-res vor!

Erika *(free)*

Er. A-lors... lan-gous-ti-nes gril-lés sau-ce aux huî-tres.

Major-domo
(in tempo)

M.-D. Lan-gous-ti-nes gril-lés sau-ce aux huî-tres.

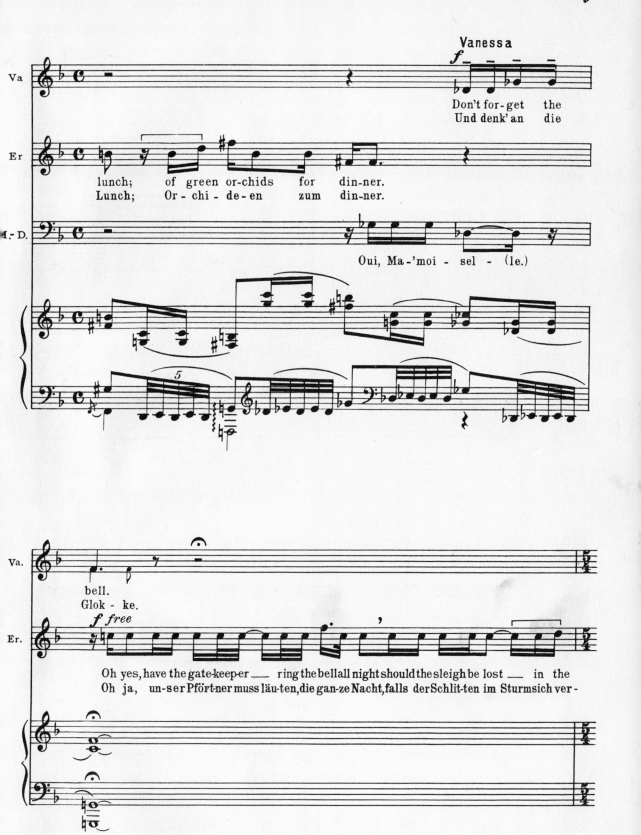

With motion ♩ = 92

Vanessa *(rising and tearing off her veil, almost anguished in her intensity)*

No, I can-not un-der-stand
Nein, ich kann es nicht ver-stehn

why he has not ar-rived yet.—
wa-rum er noch nicht da ist.—

hammered

loco

Has no mes-sage come?
Kein Be-richt bis jetzt?

Erika *(imperturbed, picks up Vanessa's veil and puts it on a chair)*

They left the vil-lage at dawn; per-haps they stopped on their way to let the storm-
Bei Dämm-rung fuhren sie ab; man hielt viel-leicht un-ter-wegs bis sich der Sturm-

Vanessa

My — guest — is not one — to let a storm stand in his
Mein — Gast — ist nicht so, — dass ihm ein Sturm seinen Weg ver-

— die down.
— ge-legt.

way and Karl should know the road — blind-fold-ed.
sperrt. Und Karl, der kennt den Weg, oh - ne Licht.

(goes to the window)

I shall have him dis-missed if they are lost.
Und ich ja - ge ihn fort, wenn er ver - sagt.

(Erika has picked up her needle-
work and sits on the couch,
calmly sewing.)

44349

13

(turns toward her mother) (For a few

Va.

E-ven now— you will not speak to me!
Und auch jetzt sprichst Du noch nicht mit mir!

(The Baroness slowly gets up, as does Erika.
Erika kisses her.)

Erika

Er.

Good night.
Gut' Nacht.

a tempo

p

seconds they look at each other in silence. Then Vanessa sits despondently on a chair near the
table. Erika, in the meantime, has pulled a bell-cord, then she slowly leads the Baroness

Va.

Go,   go;   good night.
Geh,   geh,   gut' Nacht!

f espr.

to the door; as they reach it a maid comes in and accompanies the Baroness out of the room.
Erika goes and stands by the French window which looks out on the park. Vanessa rises and
returns to her chair by the fire.)

It is a long win-ter here.
Hier ist der Win-ter— sehr lang.

Must the win-ter come so soon?
Kommt der Win-ter schon so bald?

17 (Sleighbells in the distance, *pp*, gradually increasing.)

Very fast

Lis - ten!
Hör' doch

They are
sie sind

Light up the court-yard.
Licht in den Hof-raum!

I —
Ich —

(Erika starts to run out of the room.)

— shall wait here.
— war-te hier.

And Er-i-ka,
Und E-ri-ka,

(grasping her)

let me be a-lone with him
lass mich nur al-lein mit ihm,

when he comes
wenn er her ein -

Outside are heard the bustle and turmoil of arrival, servants rushing to and fro.

She sits down by the fire with her back to the door.

Suddenly, the door is thrown open. In the semi-darkness, the figure of Anatol is seen standing silhouetted in the lighted doorway.)

to stay.
zu ban - nen!

All this _____ I have _____ done _____
All das _____ tat ich, _____ tat

(Anatol approaches her from behind, grasping her outstretched hand.)

for _____ you. _____
es für _____ Dich. _____

Oh no! ___ Poor Va-nes - sa! Aft -
Oh nein, ___ Ar-me Va-nes - sa! Nach

- er so man-y dreams, aft-er so long ___ a wait-ing!
- die-sem lan-gen Traum, nach die-sem lan - gen War-ten!

mf more sustained, but only slightly slower

Oh, how un-fair a game Life can be when
Oh, ___ wie grau-sam wird des Le - bens Spiel wenn der

Death ___ can tal-ly the score at will. ___
Tod ___ es will-kür-lich len - ken kann. ___

(He approaches the table laid for supper.)

Erika

Do not touch it; she can-not bear the sight of mir-rors.
Nicht be-rüh-ren; Sie kann kei-nen Spie-gel mehr se-hen.

Anatol

Was the sup-per laid for him?
War die Mahl-zeit hier für ihn?

41 Moderate, with grace ♩ = 66
(picking up a bottle of wine)

poco f

Ah, Ro-ma-née Con-ti!
Ah, Ro-ma-née Con-ti!

mf (nonchalantly)

My fa-ther loved this wine. May I light the can-dles?
Mein Va-ter trank ihn gern. Darf ich Licht an-zün-den?

44349

(While lighting them he reflects.)

An.

I, too, love good food and wine, but my
Auch ich lie-be gu-ten Wein. A-ber mein

fa-ther lost his for - tune dreaming, while my mother bought sub-tle
Vater ver-lor sein Geld mit Träu-men, wäh-rend Mut-ter sich Gift ver -

poi-sons to de-stroy his dreams.
schaffte, sei-nen Traum zu tö - ten.

(laughing lightly)

43

f free

An.

pect - ed.___
war - tet.___

I am the false Di - mi - tri,___ the Pre -
Ich bin der falsche Di - mi - tri, der Prä - ten -

(kneels with comic exaggeration and offers her the flower from his lapel)

a tempo

An.

ten - der; be my Ma - ri - - - na!
dent;___ sei Du Ma - ri - - - na!

sf   *espr.*   *p sub.*

f

(throwing over his shoulder the flower she has not taken)

pp

An.

You nev - er
Ihr lä - chelt

mp

poco f   *dim.*

pp

(He rises and takes her hand, leading her slowly to the table. She follows, fascinated and reluctant.)

smile._____
nie._____

44

Warm, with tender motion ♩ = 96

(Erika sits down.)

Sit down._
Nehmt Platz._

(He turns down the lamp.)

This   is   a   wild   and
Das   ist   ein   wil - der,

Scene 2

(The same. A month later on a sunny Sunday morning. A breakfast table is laid in the jardin d'hiver where, through the gleaming panes of glass, one sees the distant park covered with snow. The Baroness and Erika are sitting in the main room.)

Baroness
...and then?
...und dann?

(Curtain)

Erika *(standing by the Baroness, but looking away from her)*

He made me drink too much wine.   I showed him to his room.   I stayed with him all night.
Er gab — mir zu viel Wein.   Ich zeig - te ihm sein Zimmer.   Ich blieb bei ihm, die ganze Nacht.

The on - ly   night.
Die ei - ne   Nacht.

Baroness

The ver - y night you   met him?
Die Nacht — der Be - geg-nung?

1

I was nei-ther proud nor pure that night:
Ich war we-der stolz noch rein, die Nacht:

E-ri-ka, E-ri-ka, you so proud, so pure!
E-ri-ka, E-ri-ka, Du so stolz, so rein!

— once he kissed me it seemed so nat-u-ral to o-
— nur ein Kuss und dann muss-te ich ihm zu Wil-len

bey.
sein.

What could you have seen in such a man?
Was hast Du in die-sem Mann ge-sehn?

2 | Tempo primo ♩ = 60

Erika

If I on - ly knew | I would al - so know_____ war -
Wenn ich das nur wüsst', | ja dann wüsst' ich auch_____ war -

p espr.

cresc.

(*Erika runs to the Baroness, kneels at her feet and puts her head in her lap.*)

why I both hate and love him.
um ich ihn has - se und lie - be.

Baroness

...and now
...und jetzt,

f free

Yes, he will mar - ry me___ if I so wish;
Ja, er will mich hei - ra - ten___ wenn ich es wün - sche;

will he do the hon - or - a - ble thing?
wird er___ auch tun, was sich ge - hört?

His words are as eas-y as his kiss-es.
sein Wort ist so flüch-tig wie sein Kuss.

4 More motion

It is too late to meas-ure or to weigh;—
S'ist zu spät, um zu mes-sen und zu wä-gen;

(rises and steps away from the Baroness)

Must I? Has not each wom-an the
Muss ich? Hat denn die Frau nicht das

you must do— what must be done.
Du musst tun,— was sich ge-hört.

when our eyes meet;___ nor has the mem-'ry of that
wenn wir uns an - schaun;___ und die Er-inn-rung je-ner

night e-rased the mock-ing laugh-ter___ from his lips.
Nacht, sie nahm von sei-nen Lip-pen___ nicht den Spott.

Oh yes, oh yes, I
Oh doch, ich lie-be

Baroness

You do not love him, then?
Du liebst ihn al-so nicht?

then, Grand-moth-er, to hold what I feel is of small worth, have I the
dann, Gross-mut-ter, be-halt ich was mir nicht viel wert scheint, ist's dann nicht

f dry

(One hears the laughter of Vanessa in the jardin d'hiver.)

free

right to break an-oth-er wo-man's heart?
Un-recht, ei - ner an-dern Herz zu bre-chen?

Baroness *f free*

Whose heart?
Wes-sen Herz?

in tempo, faster

pp

(rises) f free p f sost.

Hers, of course. Have you not no-ticed? She loves him more than I do be-cause she loves him blind-ly.
Ih-res doch! Merkst Du denn gar nichts? Sie liebt ihn mehr als ich,— denn sie liebt ihn blind-lings.

The
Die

(Vanessa and Anatol, in skating togs, appear in the jardin d'hiver, carrying their skates and still laughing.)

9

Very fast and light ♪. = 100

fool!
När-rin!

Vanessa *(ringing a bell-cord for the servants)*

free

No,   you   are   not   as good a skat-er   as your fa - ther was!
Nein,   Du   bist   kein   so gu-ter Läu-fer, wie Dein Va - ter war!

Anatol

free

But I'm a luck-ier   man, per-haps.
Da-rum viel-leicht viel glück - li-cher.

(They come into the main room. During the following dialogue they will be taking off their

scarves, boots etc., which will then be collected by the Major-domo.)

Good morn - ing, E - ri - ka,   why did - n't you join us?
Gu-ten Mor-gen, E - ri -ka,   wa-rum kamst Du nicht mit uns?

Be - cause ___ you for - got to
Weil   Ihr ___ mich ___ nicht ge -

ask   me.
fragt   habt.

Did I?   Ah,   good morn-ing,   Bar-on-ess.
Wirk-lich?   Ah,   gu-ten Mor-gen, Ba-ro-nin.

Save your breath: she has be - come so old that she
Spar' den Gruss: sie ist halt jetzt so alt, dass sie

(The Doctor enters, greeting Erika.)

on - ly un - der - stands the lan - guage of the
heut' nur noch die Spra - che der Jug - end ver -

young.
steht.

(A butler has entered with a bunch of flowers which Erika places in various vases.)

(The Doctor stands, holding his pipe and reminiscing. Vanessa returns from the jardin d'hiver *with a cup of coffee.)*

in tempo, sustained

Vanessa *p free* (reflecting) ♩ = 100

Doctor
(in a leisurely manner)
mf free

Yes, dear Doc-tor.— Per-haps the day is
Ja, lie-ber Dok-tor vieHeicht kommt bald der

Ah, how good it is— to see this house a-live a-gain!
Ah, wie schön ist es, wenn hier mal wie-der Le-ben herrscht.

a tempo ♩ = 112

18

(He begins to dance with Vanessa.)

Dr.

mf

"Un - der the wil - low tree   two doves cry,   two — doves cry,
"Un - ter dem Wei - den - baum,   zwei Tau - ben,   zwei Tau-ben schrein,

p sub.

Dr.

p

Un - der the wil - low tree   two doves cry,   ah — oh!
Un - ter dem Wei - den - baum,   zwei Tau-ben schrein   ah — oh!

mp cresc.

Dr.

mf   *p*

Where shall we sleep, my love, with - er shall   we fly? Where shall we sleep, my
Wo schla-fen wir, mein Lieb, wo - hin flie - gen wir? Wo schla-fen wir, mein

mf   *p*

19

Dr.

mf

love, with - er shall we fly? _____   The wood   has swal -
Lieb, wo - hin flie-gen wir? _____   Der Wald,   der hat den

mf

- lowed the moon, the fog has swal - lowed the shore, the green toad has ___
Mond ver-schlun-gen, im Dunst ver- schwand ___ das U - fer, die Krö - te hat ver-

Anatol

20

Ah, charm-ing, charm-ing;
Ah, rei - zend, rei - zend;

swal - lowed ___ the key to my door."
schlun-gen ___ den Schlüs-sel mei - ner Tür."

I wish I could com-pete with you, Doc-tor.
O könnt' ich's doch so gut, wie Sie, Dok-tor.

Non - sense,___ young man;
Un-sinn, jun-ger Mann,

The Doctor's words may be changed to fit the particular dance-steps used.

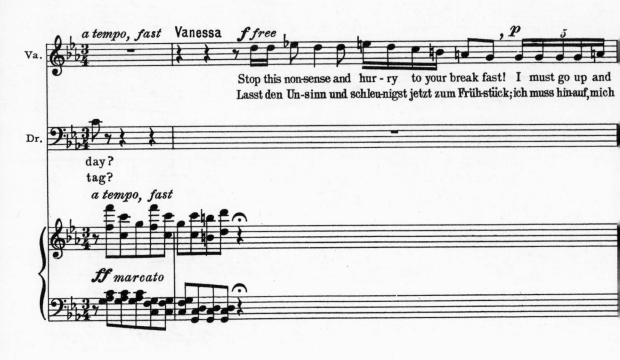

a tempo, fast **Vanessa** *ff free*

Stop this non-sense and hur - ry to your break fast! I must go up and
Lasst den Un-sinn und schleu-nigst jetzt zum Früh-stück; ich muss hin-auf, mich

day?
tag?

a tempo, fast

ff marcato

27 Waltz tempo, moving ♩=120

(Vanessa takes her muff and starts to go to her room.)

change.
um-ziehn.

*(The Doctor takes Anatol
by the arm and they start
toward the jardin d'hiver.)*

Doctor
(on the way out)

Do you play a good game of chess, sir?
Sind Sie ein gu-ter Schach-spie-ler?

Waltz tempo, moving ♩=120

p dolce

mf

fooled by a name.
irr durch den Na-men.

It is an-oth-er man _who has come.
Es ist ein an-drer Mann, der jetzt kam.

Vanessa

No, E - ri - ka. He car-ries his fa-ther's des-ti-ny with him_ and he knows it, he knows it!_
Nein, E - ri - ka. Er trägt sei-nes Va-ters Schick-sal mit sich und er weiss es, er weiss es!_

31 **As before, fiery** ♩ = 92

Ha, ha, ha, what a cu-rious niece I have!
Ha, ha, ha, Was hab' ich für ei-ne neu-gie-ri-ge Nich-te!

(She goes toward the jardin d'hiver where the young Pastor has just arrived and is seen conversing with the Doctor and Anatol.)

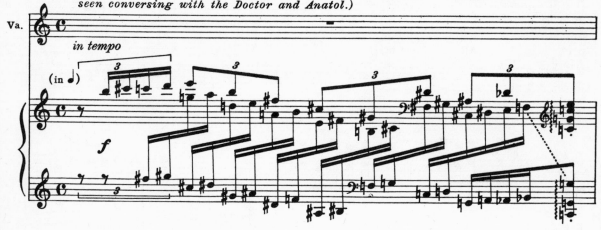

Vanessa

Dear me, here is the Pas-tor; I must hur-ry.
Mein Gott, da ist der Pfar-rer, ich muss ei-len.

Good morn-ing, Pas-tor, we shall soon be read-y.
Gu-ten Tag, Herr Pas-tor, wir sind auch gleich fer-tig.

Slower and sustained ♩ = 100

42 *(She re-enters the room*

Have some cof-fee with us.
Trinkt Kaf-fee — mit uns.

and exits inside)

mf with motion

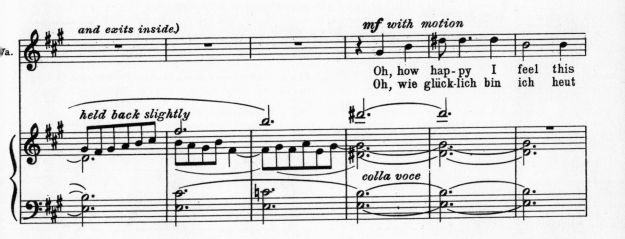

Oh, how hap-py I feel this
Oh, wie glück-lich bin ich heut

held back slightly

colla voce

morn - ing, _____ how ___ hap - - - -
mor - gen _____ wie ___ glück - - - -

- py! _____
- lich! _____

(Erika silently observes Vanessa's departure and then runs
and embraces her grandmother, who has watched the pre-

-*ceding without visible emotion.*)

Erika

Did you hear her?
Hast Du sie ge-hört?

Baroness

You must speak out
Du musst jetzt spre - chen

It is his
Ich will nur

— or you will lose him.
— o-der Du ver - lierst ihn.

love ——— I want and not his — cap-ture.
Lieb' ——— von ihm, und nicht Un-ter - wer-fung.

dy - - - - ing_____ of love?
seh - - - - ne_____ nach Lie -

espr.

be?

51 Very fast ♪ = 152

(Anatol, a coffee cup in his hand, runs into the

ff sub.

p

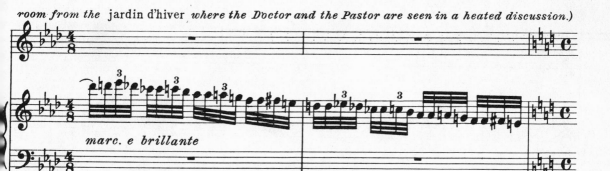

room from the jardin d'hiver *where the Doctor and the Pastor are seen in a heated discussion.)*

marc. e brillante

Er.

An.
_ be - gins to clam - or _ for her an - - swers.
_ be - ginnt zu drin - gen _ sie will Ant - wort.

slower *p* *rall.* [55] *a tempo*

Er.
I _ have the right _ to claim them! _
Ich _ hab' ein Recht auf Ant - wort! _

mf

An.
Have you not told me _
Hast Du nicht ge-sagt, ich _

slower *rall.* *a tempo*

pp *mf* *p*

Er.
p
Of
Ge -

Bar.
Baroness *pp*
Lis - ten to him, E - ri - ka;
Hör' doch auf ihn, E - ri - ka;

An.
_ I am free?
_ wä - re frei?

course, of course.
wiss, ge - wiss,

I shall not bind you____ if
Ich will Dich nicht bin - den,____ wenn

be pa - tient____ with him!
hab Nach - sicht____ mit ihm!

you are not bound by mem - 'ries.____
Dich nicht Er - inn - rung bin - det.____

56

Baroness

That night!
Je - ne Nacht!

(rises and goes to Erika)
Anatol *mf*

How could I for - get that night?
Wie könnt' ich die Nacht ver - ges - sen?

the night that
Die Nacht, die

p sub.

What a sen - ti - men - tal child you are!
Was für ein sen - ti - men - ta - les Kind Du bist!

You be-long to an-oth-er
Du ge-hörst ei - ner an-dern

Has then the hu - man heart so changed?
Hat sich das Men-schen - herz so ver-än -

age.
Zeit.

dert?

(She sits on a chair.)

(Erika abandons herself to him.)

An.

geth - er! _____ E - ri - ka! _____
sam - men! _____ E - ri - ka! _____

espr.

pp   *mf*

An.

Do you know Par - is   and Rome, ___ Bu - da - pest ___   and Vi -
Kennst Du Pa - ris ___   und Rom, ___ Bu - da - pest ___   und

mf

fp

(She rises and moves away from him, as if to escape him.)

without ritard.   63 Con moto   *p*

An.

en - na? _____ The vel - vet rooms for jew - e led   sup - pers,   the
Wien? _____ Die seidnen Räu - me zum sou - pie - ren,   die

without ritard.

p

(following her)

coast of Spain for sol- i - tude, the gild-ed Grand Ho-tels for danc-ing,
Ein-sam-keit an Spa-niens Meer, die gold-nen Grand - ho-tels zum tan-zen,

graceful

allarg. molto *a tempo* *(embracing her)*

(b) *pp*

the glass and mar-ble sta - tions for good - byes?
die Glas und Mar-mor-bahn- hofs-hal-len zum Leb - wohl?

cresc. molto

espr. *mf* *pp* *espr.*

64

f *(releasing her)*

This we could share to-geth-er if you ac-cept my love
Das hät-ten wir ge-mein-sam, wenn Du mich jetzt er - hörst

f marc. *espr.*

(Erika is suddenly wounded by his last phrase.)

Erika

Ah, _____ what a
Oh, _____ wie_

mea-ger of - fer yours is!
spär-lich ist Dein An - trag!

Lively ♩=100

- ry now!
- let euch!

sempre stacc.

mf

Let us not keep the dear Pas-tor
Las-sen wir doch den Pas-tor nicht

(She pulls a bell-cord.) 69 *(approaching the Baroness)*

mf

wait - ing.
war - ten.

Here is your shawl,
Hier ist Dein Shawl,

ff

moth-er, _____ and your prayer-book.
Mut-ter, _____ und Dein Ge - bet-buch.

stacc.

poco *f*

Anatol 73
(offering his arm to Vanessa)

An.

May I take your arm,_____ Bar - on-ess?_____
Bit-te Ih - ren Arm _____ Ba - ro-ness?

Bell

sost. Ped.

Vanessa *mp molto espr.* *(with elegance)*

Va.

You must call me Va - nes - sa.
Bit - te nenn' mich Va - nes - sa.

(They also walk out into the jardin d'hiver and disappear in the direction of the chapel. The servants follow.)

Va.

f pp

mf dim. poco a poco

pp

74 Slowly, with deep feeling ♩ = 50

(Erika, left alone, walks around the room in hysterical anguish.)

(As if to follow the others, she goes toward the jardin

d'hiver *but returns to the middle of the room and begins to pace nervously back and forth.)*

75

(She climbs up on a chair before the picture which hangs over the mantelpiece.

With a quick motion,

returning to....

she uncovers a portrait of Vanessa in a ball-dress, in all the pride of her youth.)

80 same tempo, but fast and joyous ♩=60

SOPRANO

In morn-ing light let us re-joice, Thy love is our sal-
Im Mor-gen-licht wir freu'n uns all', dass Dei-ne Lieb' uns

ALTO

TENOR

In morn-ing light let us re-joice, Thy love is our sal-
Im Mor-gen-licht wir freu'n uns all', dass Dei-ne Lieb' uns

BASS

same tempo, but fast and joyous ♩=60

(From outside one hears the strains of the first hymn coming from the chapel.)

ORGAN
(off-stage)

same tempo, but fast and joyous ♩=60

(Erika descends from the chair and backs away, her eyes always fixed on the portrait.)

Let Va - nes - sa __ have you,
Soll Va - nes - sa Dich ha - ben,

she who for so lit - tle had to wait so
sie, die für so we - nig muss - te war - ten so

84 Very fast ♩= 132

(Sobbing hysterically, she throws herself on the sofa.)

long! _____
lang! _____

Act II

(New Years Eve. Entrance hall to the castle. At the right, a stairway leading to the rooms upstairs. At the back, a very large archway through which one sees part of the ballroom. At the left, the main entrance to the castle. When the curtain goes up, the entrance hall is almost empty except for a few guests, who are greeting each other on their way into the ballroom, Nicholas, the Major-domo, who is arranging all the fur coats, cloaks, hats, etc., on racks by the door, and a footman, who is standing at the entrance of the ballroom. In the ballroom, from which is heard the hum of conversation, one sees couples dancing to an off-stage orchestra.)

*(More guests descend the stairway and
are greeted as they enter the ballroom. Nicholas opens the door and helps a couple of*

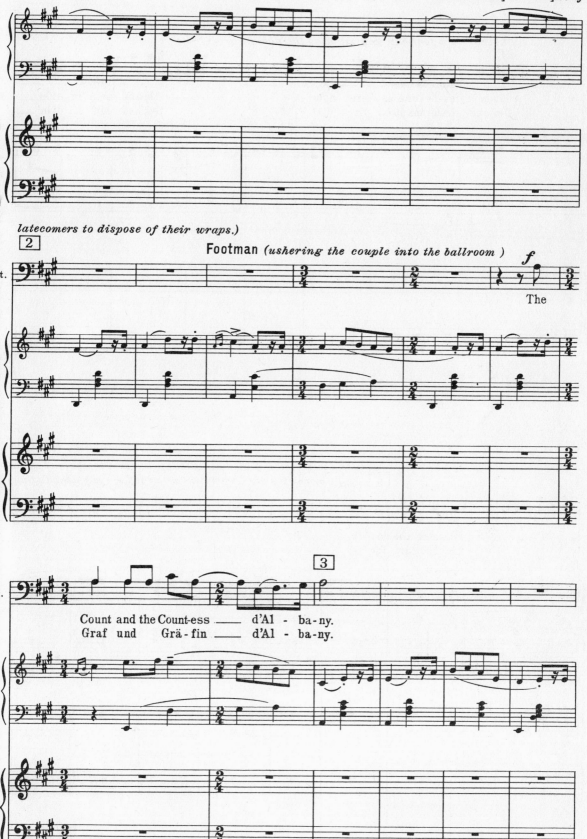

latecomers to dispose of their wraps.)

Footman *(ushering the couple into the ballroom)*

The

Count and the Count-ess ____ d'Al - ba-ny.
Graf und Grä - fin ____ d'Al - ba-ny.

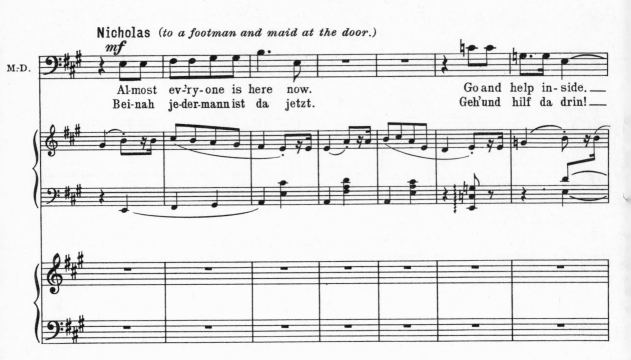

Nicholas *(to a footman and maid at the door.)*

Al-most ev'ry-one is here now.
Bei-nah je-der-mann ist da jetzt.

Go and help in-side. ___
Geh'und hilf da drin! ___

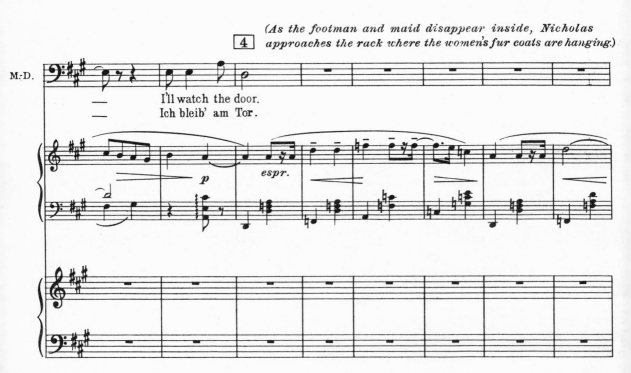

(As the footman and maid disappear inside, Nicholas approaches the rack where the women's fur coats are hanging.)

I'll watch the door.
Ich bleib' am Tor.

Ah,　these love - ly　furs...
Ah,　schön so ein　Pelz...

(He rubs his cheek against one of them with a deep sigh.)

(The Doctor, a little tipsy, comes in from the

so soft,　so
so weich,　so

ballroom holding two glasses of champagne. He looks at Nicholas in great astonishment.)

M.-D.

sweet-ly scent- ed.   This is all I shall ev- er
himm-lich duf-tend.   Das ist al-les, was ich je-mals

M.-D.

know of such wom- en. _____
von sol-chen Fraun er - fah - - - re.

7 Doctor

Dr.

You ras-cal, you!
Du Spitz-bub, Du!

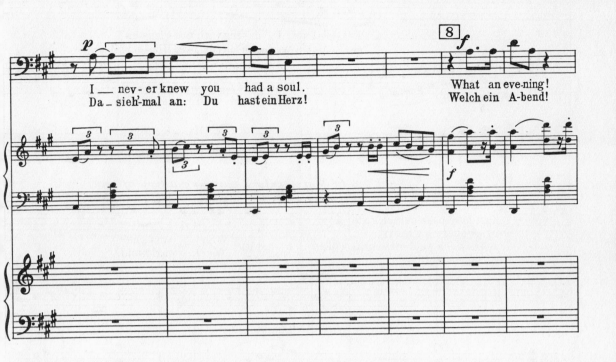

I — nev-er knew you had a soul.
Da _ sieh'-mal an: Du hast ein Herz!

What an eve-ning!
Welch ein A-bend!

What — wom - en,
Was für Frau - en!

what cham - pagne!
Und Cham - pag -

But what am I do-ing with *two* glass-es?
ner! A-ber was mach'ich mit *zwei* Glä-sern?

(spoken)
I must have been carrying one
to some charming lady:
Eines hab' ich wohl einer charmanten
Dame geben wollen.

(A lackey enters, carrying a tray of empty glasses.) *f* (sung)

Who was she?
Wer war's wohl?

(He drinks both glasses himself, then follows the lackey and attempts to put the glasses on the tray. He misses it and the glasses crash to the

Oh well...
Na schön...

floor; a lackey picks up the pieces disapprovingly and exits.)

(spoken)

Sorry!
Schade!

(sighs)

mf free

I should nev-er have been a doc-tor, Nich-o-las;
Weisst Du, ich hät-te kein — Dok-tor wer-den sol-len;

a gen-tle-man, a po-et, that's what I am.
ein Gent-le-man, ein Dich-ter, ja, das bin ich.

Slower ♩ = 60

A na-ked bod-y,
Ein nack-ter Kör-per,

what is it to a doc-tor?
was sagt das ei-nem Dok-tor?

We see them ev-'ry day.
Das sehn wir je-den Tag.

11

p held back, then moving ahead with increasing gusto

But un-der a chan-de-lier, with the right mu-sic, the right
Doch un-ter dem Kron-leuch-ter, mit der Ball-mu-sik, das Par-

cresc. poco a poco

140

44349

(Two maids are seen on the stairway, giggling at the Doctor.)

(confidentially to Nicholas)

Did you see me dance — with Ma'-moi - selle Do-riat?
Hast Du mich tan-zen sehn — mit Ma'-moi - selle Do-riat?

She's not so young, ——— I know that,
Sie ist nicht so jung, ——— ich weiss das,

a bit too plump, per - haps, a bit too tall* for
et-was zu plump, viel - leicht, et-was zu gross* für

(with delight)

me. But, oh, so light — on her feet,
mich. Doch oh, die tanzt auf leich-tem Fuss,

* may be changed to "small"
"klein"

head... _____

Haupt _____

("Doc-tor,   dear Doc-tor,   not

("Dok-tor,   Herr Dok-tor,   nein,

quite   so fast,   dear Doc-tor!")   her bos-om heav-ing

nicht   so schnell,   Herr Dok-tor!")   Ihr Bu-sen wogt mir

un- der my chin...(own...)   ("Doc-tor,   dear Doc-tor,   not quite so fast, dear

un- ter dem Kinn...   ("Dok-tor,   Herr Dok-tor,   nein, nicht so schnell, Herr

Doc-tor!")   Oh   la, la!

Dok-tor!")   Oh   la, la!

(losing his balance)

rall.   portamento   slightly less motion, jerkily

a tempo

Dr. I must stop drink-ing. I still have to an-nounce the en-
Jetzt Schluss mit Trin-ken. Ich muss ja die Ver-lo-bung noch ver-

18 Quieter ♩ = 100

Dr. gage-ment. Yes, Nich-o-las, yes,
kün-den. Ja, Ni-cho-las, ja,—

(affectionately)

Dr. they chose the old fam-i-ly doc-tor— to make the an-
der gu-te al-te On-kel Dok-tor,— der muss es ver-

19

Dr. nounce-ment. A sweet i-dea... ver-y touch-ing,
kün-den. Net-te I-dee. Wirk-lich rüh-rend,

(feeling in his coat pockets)

rall.

ver - y touch-ing.
wirk-lich rüh-rend.

Good heav-ens, where is my
O Him-mel, wo ist mein

free, quite fast

(Without noticing, he has dropped the text of his speech on the floor: Major-domo picks it up.)

speech?
Speech?

I should not have drunk so much; I shall mud-dle up ev-ry-thing.
Hätt'ich nur nicht so viel ge-trun-ken: ich bring jetzt al-les durch-ein-an-der.

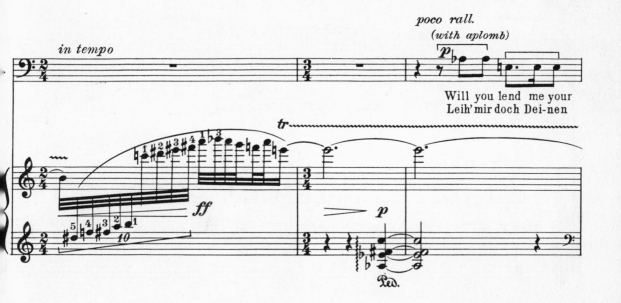

in tempo

poco rall.
(with aplomb)

Will you lend me your
Leih'mir doch Dei-nen

She will not o - pen the door for me, she will not an-swer.
Mir macht sie ein-fach die Tür nicht auf, Ant - wort gibt sie nicht.

Faster, as before ♩ = 120 Doctor

I will see what I can do.
Ich ver - su - che, was ich kann.

23 *(going upstairs and talking to himself as he runs out of breath)* *mf*

("Doc - tor, dear Doc-tor,
("Dok - tor, Herr Dok-tor,

poco rall. *pp* *(exits)*

not quite so fast, dear Doc - tor!")
nein, nicht so schnell, Herr Dok - tor!")

24 Anatol *(enters from the ballroom)*

Moving gently ♩=80

At last I've found you.
Find' ich Dich end - lich.

What is wrong, Va-nes-sa?
Was is los, Va-nes-sa?

(Vanessa sits on the steps and covers her face with her hands as if she were about to cry.)

25 Agitated, with motion ♩.=63

Vanessa

I feel so weak, — A-na-tol, —
Ich fühl' mich schwach, A-na-tol, —

so a-fraid.
ha-be Angst.

Why will not those two come down?
Ah, die kom-men nicht her-un-ter,

Anatol

A - fraid of what, my dar-ling?
Angst — wo-vor, mein Lieb-ling?

152

44349

Doppio mosso

(She buries her head on his shoulder.)
allarg. molto

Is there some-thing you have not told me, A - na-tol?
Hast Du mir denn et-was ver-schwie-gen, A - na-tol?

dim. poco a poco

28 With quiet motion ♩ = 76
Anatol

Love has a bit-ter core,____ Va - nes - sa.____
Lie - be hat bit-tren Kern,____ Va - nes - sa.____

con Ped.

Do not taste too deep,____ Va - nes - sa.____
spü - re nicht zu tief,____ Va - nes - sa.____

espr.

simile, legato sempre

154

44349

Love has a bit-ter core, A-na-tol, but let me taste
Lie - be hat bit-tren Kern, A-na-tol, doch lass' mich spüren

gun.
an.

this bit-ter-ness with you. I shall nev - er take too much
die Bit-ter-keit mit Dir. Ich be-hal - te nie zu viel,

if you will of-fer all,
wenn Du mir al - les schenkst,

Anatol

Do not search in-to the
Su - che nicht in dem, was

somewhat broader
f

For you,— A-na-tol,— for you.— Like the burn-ing
Auf Dich,— A-na-tol,— auf Dich.— Wie der flam-men-de

on— ly born that night.
Welt in je-ner Nacht.

marcato
poco *f*
mf

moving ahead . . . to . . . tempo (♩ = 66)

phoe-nix you soared————— out— of the ash-es of my
Phö-nix so stiegst————— Du— aus der A-sche mei-ner

fp *fp*

shat-tered— dreams.
ster-ben-den Träu - me.

36 **With increasing motion** ♩=76

Anatol
p

Then scat-ter the ash-
Ver-streu-e die A-

With increasing motion ♩=76
fp
f

Call our peo-ple in; have them stand by the door.
Ruft die Leu-te her, stellt sie dort an die Tür;

They should be-gin their danc-es right af-ter the an-nounce-ment.
und be-ginnt mit den Tän-zen so-fort nach der Ver-kün-dung.

41 Dance tempo as before ♩=160
(*She goes inside the ballroom. Major-domo exits by a small side door.*)

Orchestra
(off-stage)

Dance-tempo as before ♩=160
brillante

(Guests are dancing in the ballroom.)

Anatol

(to the Doctor, while following Vanessa)

An.

mp

What did she real-ly say?
Was sag- te sie wirk-lich?

Doctor

p

42 *(They go inside the ballroom.*

Dr.

She would not speak_____ to me.
Sie sprach kein Wort_____ mit mir.

A group of peasants, including a violinist, an accordionist and a group of children is ushered in by a lackey. They cross the hall and stand by the door leading into the ballroom, making a solid wall with their backs to the audience.*

43 *Suddenly Erika, in a white ball dress, appears at the top of the staircase; she seems weak and very pale, desperately battling to master herself.*

Same tempo, but quieter

* The violinist may be a child.

45 *After a little hesitation she begins to descend the stairs.*

As the music inside fades, only the hum of conversation is heard.)

46

(At the sound of the Doctor's voice, Erika stops short, halfway down the stairway, as if suddenly taken very ill, She clutches her stomach.)

Doctor (inside ballroom)

Dr.

Si-lence, ev-'ry-bod-y, si-lence, please.
Ru-he mei-ne Herrschaften, Ru-he bit-te!

La-dies and gentlemen,
Mei-ne Da-men und Herr'n,

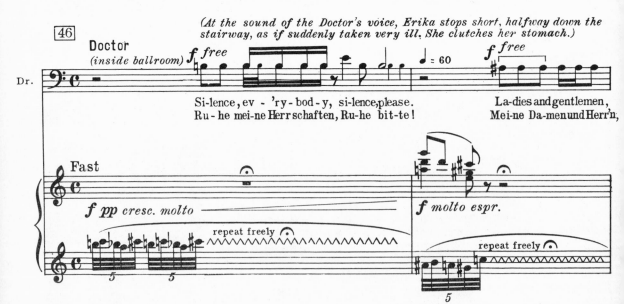

(spoken)

I have the great honor, as an old friend of this noble and distinguished family, which for many years has been a shining example to all of us of what is finest in the traditions of our country to announce the engagement of our dear Baroness Vanessa von...

(gesprochen)

Ich habe die grosse Ehre, als alter Freund dieser noblen und vornehmen Familie, die viele Jahre lang ein leuchtendes Beispiel für uns alle dafür war, was in der Tradition unsres Landes als Bestes gilt, die Verlobung anzuzeigen unsrer lieben Baroness Vanessa von...

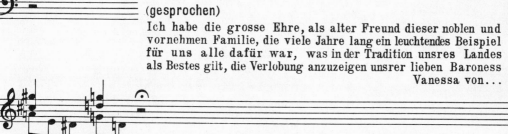

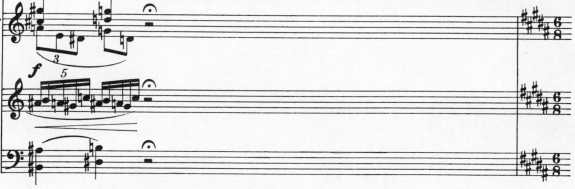

(The orchestra drowns out the last words of the Doctor. Erika suddenly faints on the steps.)

stringendo

allarg. molto

Doctor *(Applause is heard inside.)* *f free*

Dr.

Now let us drink to the hap-py cou-ple!
Nun lasst uns trin-ken auf das jun-ge Paar!

Very fast ♩= 160

(Vanessa and Anatol appear from the ball-room; Vanessa is carrying a tray of sweets for the peasant children.)

ff

Chorus *(inside)*

SOPRANO *ff*

Now to your
Auf Eu - er

ALTO *ff*

TENOR *ff*

Now to your
Auf Eu - er

BASS *ff*

(Accordion on stage)

ff

gliss.

Like a folk-dance ♩ = 152

49 *(One of the peasant children does a dance and the violinist and accordionist play upstage right, so that in watching them, everyone is facing away from the steps where Erika is lying.)*

health! _____
Wohl! _____

health! _____
Wohl! _____

Like a folk-dance ♩ = 152

non legato

Like a folk-dance ♩ = 152

(violin on-stage)

f

8---

50

f

Pro-sit,   pro-sit,   pro - - sit!

f

Pro-sit,   pro-sit,   pro - - sit!

f

take place, the Major-domo enters the hall from the ballroom.)

(The peasants, musicians,*
guests, Vanessa and Anatol
drift back into the ballroom.)

(On seeing Erika, Nicholas rushes up the stairs.)

52 **Suddenly slower as before** ♩ = 120

pp

Un - der the wil - low tree   two   doves   cry,   two___
Un - ter dem Wei - den - baum   zwei   Tau - ben,   zwei___

pp

Un - der the wil - low tree   two   doves   cry,
Un - ter dem Wei - den - baum   zwei   Tau   -   ben,

pp

Un - der the   wil   -   low tree   two   doves cry,   two___
Un - ter dem   Wei   -   den - baum   zwei   Tau - ben,   Tau -

pp

Un - der the   wil   -   low tree   two   doves cry,   two___
Un - ter dem   Wei   -   den - baum   zwei   Tau - ben,   Tau -

Suddenly slower as before ♩ = 120

pp

(The Major-domo leaves her reluctantly.)

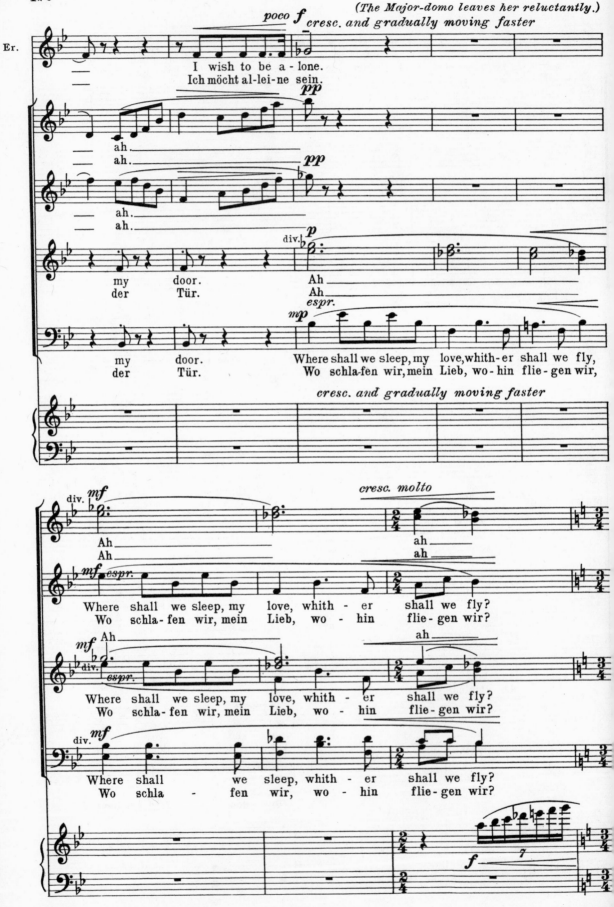

62

(The Baroness, dishevelled and clad in an old dressing gown, appears at the top of the stairway.)

Baroness **63**

E - ri-ka!   E - ri-ka!   Where are you go - ing,

E - ri-ka!   E - ri-ka!   Wo-hin gingst Du,

some - one...
Leu - te...
E -
E -

66

(The dances in the ballroom continue.)

(suddenly entering)

What are you do-ing here?
Was hast Du hier zu su-chen?

ri - ka!
ri - ka!

E - ri - ka..
E - ri - ka..

Orch.
off-stage   *f*   insolently

44349

67 *(The dancing and*

Van.

Are you out of your mind?
Bist Du völ-lig von Sin-nen?

Bar.

E - ri - ka!___
E - ri - ka!___

An.

(Anatol has followed Vanessa into

laughter inside have stopped and a few groups of dancers come into the hall in amazement.)

the hall.) **f**

E - ri - ka!   What of E - ri - ka?
E - ri - ka!   Wo ist E - ri - ka?

She must be saved...
Man muss sie ret-ten...

Act III
Scene I

(Erika's bedroom. A few hours later. At one side of the room, a small alcove in which part of the bed is seen. It is dawn.)

3 Very fast ♩ = 144

slightly slower, freely

(*The Baroness is sitting by a small fireplace with her back to the audience. The Doctor is standing by a window, peering out anxiously through the panes. Vanessa, in a dressing gown, is pacing nervously up and down the room. Cries and calls and barking of dogs are heard outside.*)

Moderato ♩ = 80

E-ri-ka, E-ri-ka,_ what made you do this?
E-ri-ka, E-ri-ka,_ sag', wa-rum tatst Du's?

(to the Doctor)

You are her doc-tor_
Sie sind ihr Dok-tor_

_ and her life-long friend. Is it pos-si-ble you sus-pect-ed noth-ing?
_ und ihr al-ter Freund, ist es mög-lich, dass Ih-nen gar nichts auf-fiel?

Doctor

I have al-ways known I am a bad doc-tor: now I
Ich hab's ja ge-wusst, ich bin ein schlech-ter Dok-tor: und jetzt

It may all be ver-y in-no-cent.
Es kann al-les ja ganz harm-los sein.

They found no trace of her steps near the lake and the ice was un-bro-ken.
Und man fand auch kei-ne Spur bei dem See und das Eis nicht ge-bro-chen.

9 Broader ♩ = 50
Vanessa

Why must the great-est sor - rows come from
Die schaf-fen uns das gröss - te Leid, die

those we most love?
wir am meis-ten lie - ben.

(The Doctor goes over to the Baroness to reassure her, then quickly exits. Vanessa rings for the servants and begins to prepare the bed in the alcove.)

(The door of the bedroom is thrown open and Erika is carried in by Anatol, a group of peasants and ball guests, followed by the Doctor. They place her, still wearing her ball dress, on the bed in the alcove.)

An.

You will find wine down-stairs___ and a blaz-ing fire___ in the kitch-en.
Un-ten gibt es zu trin-ken und das Feu-er brennt in der Kü-che.

(The peasants tiptoe out of the room followed a little later by the guests. The Doctor remains in the alcove with Vanessa. Two maids enter hurriedly and go into the alcove to help un-dress Erika and put her to bed. Care should be taken, however, that Erika, sheltered by the figures of the maid and the Doctor, remains unseen by the audience.)

Vanessa *(coming out of the alcove and leaning against Anatol, who embraces her tenderly)*

Va.

Oh, in what ter-ror___ I have been! An-a-tol, An-a-tol...
Oh, wel-chen Schrek-ken___ stand ich aus! A-na-tol, A-na-tol...

Anatol *(Vanessa bursts into tears.)*

An.

With motion ♪ = 80

Poor Va-nes-sa, what an end-less night!
Ar-me Va-nes-sa, so ei-ne end-lo-se Nacht!

An. small ra - vine __ like a wound - ed bird.
klei - nen Schlucht __ wie ein wun - der Vo - gel.

mp

Ped. **Ped.** **Ped.** **Ped.**

An. She must have fal - len for her frost - white dress was
Sie war wohl ge - fal - len, denn ihr Kleid war ganz zer -

Ped. **Ped.** **Ped.** **Ped.**

An. torn and damp with blood. __
ris - sen und feucht von Blut. __

Ped. **Ped.** **Ped.** **Ped.**

25 *mf* *espr., with more voice* *mp*

An. There she lay __ in the snow __ like a Christ - mas ro - se; the bit - ter
Da __ lag sie __ in dem Schnee, wie ei - ne Weih - nachts - ro - se, ihr süss; Ge -

mf *3* *p*

sempre con pedale

cold   had glazed her love - ly   face   in - to deep   and o - paque
sicht   war ganz von Frost ver - eist,   so als läg'   sie in tie - fem

sleep.   The faint beat _ of her heart   was like an un - de -
Schlaf.   Ihr Herz - schlag war so schwach   und wie ein un - be -

ci - phered sig - nal _   from an - oth - er world.
kann - tes Zei - chen _   aus der   an - dern Welt.

Ossia   back _ to _

I lift - ed her in - to my   arms, warmed her _ a - gainst my   breast.
Ich hob sie auf   in meinen   Arm, wärmt sie _ an mei - ner   Brust.

(He gently accompanies them outside, closing the door softly behind them. There is a long silence in the room. The Baroness, seated by Erika, still has not moved.)

very sustained

espr.

poco f

Erika *(from inside the alcove)*

allarg.

35 **Slowly and very simply** ♩ = 42

Grand-moth-er!__
Gross-mut-ter!__

Do they know?__
Wis-sen die?__

Baroness

Yes, E-ri-ka.
Ja, E-ri-ka.

How can I tell?__
Wie kann ich's sagen?

I was with child...
Ich er-war-te-te ein Kind...

Why did you wish to die?____
Wa-rum woll-test Du ster-ben?__

with child!
ein Kind!

dolce

Grand-moth-er, grand-
Gross-mut-ter, Gross-

- moth-er! an - swer me!
- mut-ter! sag' mir's doch!

(Without answering, the

Baroness leaves the room.)

Curtain

Intermezzo

Scene II

(The drawing room as in Act I, a month later. The Baroness is sitting in her usual place; Anatol, in traveling clothes enters upstage and goes down to speak to the Doctor who is standing by the table. A maid is in the jardin d'hiver, *packing a small suitcase. The main door at the back of the room is open. Through it one sees servants carrying trunks and other luggage across the hall.)*

By the time we ar - rive in Par - is ⸺ the new house should be read - y.
Wenn wir an - kom - men in Pa - ris ⸺ ist das neu - e Haus fer - tig.

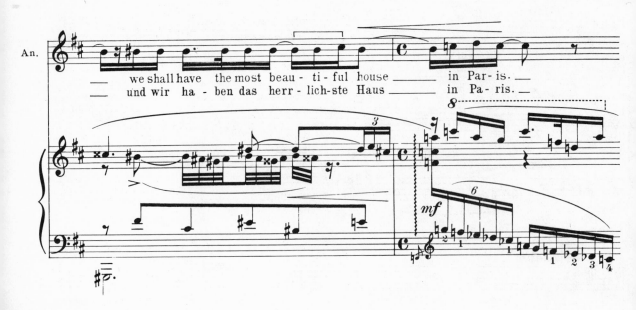

An.

we shall have the most beau - ti - ful house _____ in Par - is.
und wir ha - ben das herr - lich-ste Haus _____ in Pa - ris.

mf

(Vanessa, in travelling costume, with hat and veil, comes into the room.)

An.

Vanessa *poco f*

Va.

I am al - most read - y. _____
Ich bin bei - nah fer - tig. _____

poco f, grazioso

p

Ped. *Ped.*

40

mf free

Anatol
(kissing her.)

poco f

Be sure that they put
Pass' auf dass sie

How love - ly you look!
Wie schön siehst Du aus!

mf

p — pp

ev-e-ry-thing in the sleigh   and tell them to be care-ful with the hat   box-es.
al-les in den Schlit-ten tun, und sag ih-nen, sie sol-len be-son-ders auf die Hut-schach-teln acht-ge-ben.

(She goes out into the jardin d'hiver to help the maid pack a small suitcase. Anatol exits.)

tempo

mf

p

mumps, the chick-en pox, the scar- la - ti - na? How man-y times I kissed your burn-ing
Mumps, die Wind-pok-ken, das Schar-lach-fie-ber? Ich hab' Dir oft die heis - se Wang' ge-

hurrying a little *(with mock heroism)*

cheek and fought the grin-ning dwarfs leer-ing at the foot of your
küst, die Zwer-ge oft be-kämpft, die schiel - ten am Fuss Dei-nes

43

(Vanessa gives the maid a small farewell present. Maid

returning - - to - - Tempo I

bed! Will you ev- er
Betts! Wirst Du auch ein-

exits tearfully, carrying the suitcase.)

think_ of your old doc - tor now, now_ that the pulse of your
mal an Dei-nen al- ten Dok-tor denken? jetzt_ wo der Puls Dei-nes

Dr. heart takes you _ so far a - way _____ from him? _____
Her- zens Dich so weit ent - fernt _____ von ihm? _____

44 (*Vanessa enters from the* jardin d'hiver, *followed shortly after by Erika from the hall; the latter is simply dressed and looks very pale and tense.*)

Vanessa

p (to Doctor)

Va. And you, _ my friend, what are you mum-bling a - bout?
Und Sie, mein Freund, was mur-meln Sie vor sich hin?

A little more motion ♩ = 60

singing

stacc.

(*interrupting him*)
mp

Va. Yes, yes, _ dear Doc-tor...
Ja, ja, lie-ber Dok-tor...

mf (with tears in his voice)

Dr. Oh, my dear, I just want-ed to tell you...
Oh mein Kind, ich wollt' Ih-nen grad sa-gen...

l.h.

(She leads the Doctor gently towards the

Come, you go and help An-a-tol.
Gut... Hel-fen Sie A-na-tol.

door which she closes after him.)

45 **Faster, somewhat agitated**
♩. = 80

(Vanessa sits
on the sofa.)

E-ri-ka, sit down here next to me.
E-ri-ka, setz' Dich hier ne-ben mich.

(Erika sits next to her, but all through the scene avoids looking at her.)
tempo

and don't for-get... _____
und dann ver-giss ___ nicht...

Don't wor-ry, ___ Aunt Va - nes - sa,
Sei un-be-sorgt, ___ Va - nes - sa,

With more motion ♩ = 66
48 (uncertainly)

E-ri-ka,
E-ri-ka,

it shall all be _ as if you _ were here. _
es bleibt al - les, wie wenn Du _ da wärst. _

be-fore I leave you must tell me the truth _ a-bout that night.
be-vor ich geh', sag mir, was ist ge - schehn in je - ner Nacht.

I have told you the
Ich hab es Dir ge -

p staccatissimo

44349

236

44349

(Vanessa takes the Major-domo in her arms affectionately.)

(The Doctor comes back into the room and stops by Vanessa's side.)

(The Baroness has risen and they all stand quite motionless.)

55 **Simply, with deep feeling** ♩ = 46

leave, to break, to find, ____ to keep, to stay, to wait, to
geht, man löst, man fasst, ____ man hält, man bleibt, man harrt, man

hope, to dream, to weep and re-mem-ber. To love is all of this
hofft, man träumt, man weint im Ge-den-ken; man liebt in je-dem Fall

Anatol

To leave, to break, to
Man geht, man löst, man

and none ____ of it ____ is love. ____ The light ____ is not the
und nichts ____ da-von ist Lie-be. Das Licht ____ ist nicht die

find, ____ to keep, to stay, to wait, to
fasst, ____ man hält, man bleibt, man harrt, man

Va.

(Major-domo and a maid enter with
coats and wraps.)

we shall drop you__ in the vil - lage.__
wir neh-men Euch bis ins Dorf mit.__

Er.

Erika

mp

I shall wave good-bye__ from here.
Ich wink Euch von hier__ noch nach.

mf

63 *(Vanessa turns back and embraces Erika, then, after a last look, quickly leaves the room*
with Anatol and the Doctor. The Major-domo closes the door and Erika is left alone with
espr. *the Baroness.)*

mf

(She goes to the jardin d'hiver *and looks out into the snow.*

f

moving imperceptibly

f

8

One can see that she is making desperate efforts to control her inner agony.   At the

sound of the departing sleigh she weakly raises her hand
(Sleighbells off-stage)

(turns from the window)
(with a cry)

to wave good-bye.) Erika

An - a-tol,
A - na-tol,

(comes back into the room and leans against a chair; as if she were about to collapse; but

An - a - tol!
A - na - tol!

quickly straightens herself and with great determination goes to the wall to pull a bell-chord.)

65 With motion ♩ = 80

Er.

No, I must nev-er say that name a - gain.
Nein, die-sen Na-men spre-che ich nie mehr aus.

(The Baroness slowly moves toward her usual chair.)

Er.

Luck - y those peo-ple___ who are so anx-ious___ to be -
Glück-lich die Leu-te___ die so be-reit sind, al - les zu

Er.

lieve! Do you real-ly think she be-lieves what I said?___ Grandmother?
glau-ben! Denkst Du wirk-lich, dass sie es glaubt was ich sag - te? Grossmutter?

(The Baroness sits by the fire.)

Er.

Oh, I for-got that you will not speak to me ei - ther now.
Oh, ich ver-gass, dass Du auch mit mir nicht mehr spre-chen willst.

66 (The Major-domo comes in.)

rall. a tempo free

I am tru-ly a - lone.___ Will you please cov-er all the mir-rors in this house a-gain.
Ich bin wirk-lich al - lein ___ Bit - te dek - ken Sie al - le Spie-gel hier jetzt wie-der zu.

Yes, just as be-fore. Be-gin with these now.
Ja, grad wie vor-her. Fan-gen Sie hier an.
(Major-domo bows and exits.)

(astounded)

What, Ma'-moi-selle?
Wie, Ma'-moi-selle?

Dark and unquiet ♩ = 72

67

(Erika fetches a veil similar to the one worn by
Vanessa at the beginning of Act I.)

stacc. sempre

(The Major-domo enters from the hall, followed by a servant with a step-ladder and some

With motion ♩ = 92

68

drapes.)

Erika   *allarg.*   *mf free*

From now on I shall re-ceive no vis-i-tors.
Und jetzt em-pfang ich kei-ne Be-su-cher mehr.

approximately with the voice

Tell the gate-keep-er that the gate to the park must remain locked at all times. Thank you.
Sagt dem Tor-wäch-ter, dass das Tor in den Park im-mer ge-schlossen sein muss. Dan- ke.

As before ♩= 46
(Erika sits by the fire next to her grandmother.)

Erika

mf rall.

Ah, that is
Ah, das ist

poco rall.

cresc. espr.

sost. Ped.

(The Major-domo and lackey drape the mirror.)

Slightly slower

a tempo

Now it is my turn to wait.
Nun ist's an mir zu war -

good.
gut.

mp

pochiss. rit.

dry and staccatissimo *mp*

mp

Ped. sost. Ped.

(Erika slowly covers her head with the veil, hiding her face.)

a tempo

poco allarg.

(Curtain)

- ten.

p

pp espr.

pp

pp

Ped. Ped.

GLOSSARY OF TEMPO INDICATIONS

GLOSSARY OF TEMPO INDICATIONS

Act I

ENGLISH	GERMAN	ITALIAN
fiery	feurig	focoso
faster	schneller	più mosso
somewhat sustained	etwas mässiger	piùttosto sostenuto
again	wieder	ancora
less motion	weniger bewegt	meno mosso
dark and unquiet	dunkel und unruhig	cupo e inquieto
with grace	graziös	grazioso
with motion	mit Bewegung	con moto
slowly	langsam	lentamente
sustained, but with motion	sostenuto, aber bewegt	sostenendo, ma con moto
tranquil and sustained	ruhig (sostenuto)	tranquillo e sostenuto
a little motion, rubato	mit Bewegung, rubato	un poco mosso, rubato
fast and agitated	schnell (agitato)	presto e agitato
returning to tempo	zum Tempo zurückkehrend	tornando al tempo
a little slower	etwas langsamer	poco meno mosso
more sustained, but only slightly slower	più sostenuto aber kaum langsamer	più sostenuto ma appena più lento
slightly broader	etwas breiter	un poco più largo
a bit freely	ein bischen frei	un po' liberamente
lingering slightly	etwas zaudernd	esitando
quietly, but in tempo	ruhig, aber im Tempo	tranquillamente, in tempo
less motion	mit weniger Bewegung	meno mosso
warm, with tender motion	warm, mit zarter Bewegung	con calore e dolcemente mosso
broadening	breiter werdend	allargando

Act II

ENGLISH	GERMAN	ITALIAN
moderate tempo	In gemässigtem Zeitmass	moderato
moving	bewegt	movendo
more motion	bewegter	più mosso
moving ahead	vorwärts	incalzando poco a poco
tenderly, as before	zärtlich, wie vorher	teneramente, come prima
faster	schneller	più mosso
very fast and light	sehr schnell und leicht	molto allegro e leggero
sustained	sostenuto	sostenuto
with supple motion	mit geschmeidiger Bewegung	movendo con souplesse
moving ahead slightly	etwas bewegter	un poco movendo
back to tempo	zum Tempo zurückkehrend	tornando al tempo
gradually into Waltz tempo	allmählich zum Walzer Tempo übergehend	poco a poco a tempo di valzer
fast, with spirit	mit Schwung	allegro con spirito
with increasing intensity	mit steigender Intensität	sempre più intenso
quick and agitated	schnell und aufgeregt	presto agitato
broadening slightly	etwas breiter	poco allargando
light and debonair, with motion	leicht bewegt und debonair	leggero e bonario, con moto
hurrying a little	etwas eilend	poco affrettando

Act II (Continued)

ENGLISH	GERMAN	ITALIAN
lively	lebhaft	vivace
slowly, with deep feeling	langsam, mit tiefer Empfindung	lentamente, intensamente espressivo
always faster	immer schneller	sempre più presto
wildly	wild	con furia
calming down	ruhiger werdend	calmandosi
broadening to previous tempo	breiter werdend bis zurück ins vorherige Zeitmass	allargando, tornadando al tempo primo
same tempo, but fast and joyous	im selben Tempo, aber schnell und freudig	lo stesso tempo; con allegria

Act III

as fast as possible	so schnell wie möglich	presto possibile
increasing slightly	poco a poco crescendo	poco a poco crescendo
jaunty	keck und übermütig	baldanzoso
a tempo, a little less	in Tempo, aber etwas langsamer	a tempo, ma un po' più lento
quieter	ruhiger	più tranquillo
restless	unruhig	ansioso
moving gently	sanft fliessend	dolce e scorrevole
with quiet motion	in ruhiger Bewegung	tranquillamente
somewhat broader	etwas breiter	poco più largo
with increasing motion	immer fliessender	sempre più mosso
same tempo, but quieter	im selben Tempo, aber ruhiger	con più calmo
anguished	angstvoll	con angoscia
like a folk-dance	wie ein Volkstanz	come una danza popolare
suddenly slower as before	plötzlich ruhiger wie vorher	improvvisamente più lento come prima

Act IV

mysterious	geheimnisvoll	misterioso
without dragging	nicht schleppend	senza trascinare
flowing gently	sanft fliessend	scorrevole
slightly more motion	etwas bewegter	poco più mosso
gradually faster, with hushed excitement	allmählich schneller, mit verhaltner Erregung	poco a poco più mosso, con emozione contenuta
with growing agitation	mit wachsender Erregung	con emozione crescente
with sudden rapture	plötzlich verzückt, berauscht	con estasi improvvisa
much quieter	viel ruhiger	molto più tranquillo
slowly and very simply	langsam und sehr einfach	lentamente e semplicemente
unquiet	unruhig	inquieto
impetuous	ungestüm	impetuoso
simply, with deep feeling	einfach, mit tiefer Empfindung	semplicemente, con profonda espressione
moving freely	frei aber immer bewegt	movendo liberamente
faster, flowing moderately	schneller, mit mässigem Fluss	più presto, ma moderato
tender and sustained	zart und getragen	tenero, sostenuto
approximately with the voice	die Stimme begleitend	seguendo la voce senza rigore
slightly slower	etwas langsamer	poco più lento